How do I feel about

MY STEPFAMILY

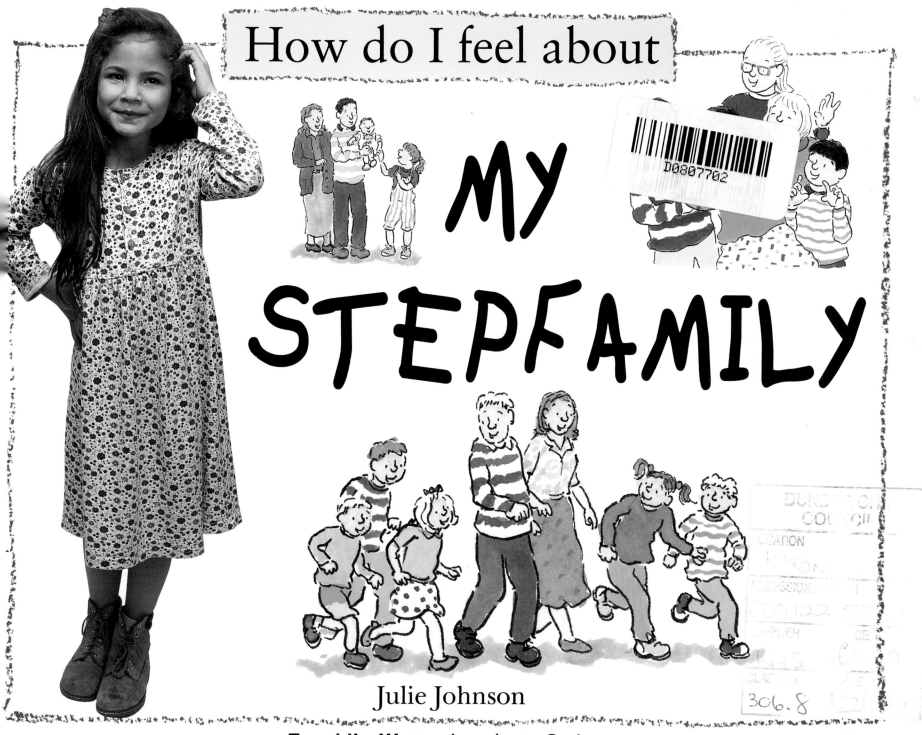

Julie Johnson

Franklin Watts London • Sydney

An Aladdin Book
© Aladdin Books Ltd 1997

All rights reserved

Designed and produced by
Aladdin Books Ltd
28 Percy Street
London W1P 0LD

First published in Great Britain
in 1997 by Franklin Watts
96 Leonard Street
London EC2A 4RH

ISBN: 0 7496 2669 0 (hb)
ISBN: 0 7496 3629 7 (pb)

A catalogue record for this
book is available from the
British Library.

Printed in Belgium

Designer   Tessa Barwick
Editor   Sarah Levete
Illustrator   Christopher
               O'Neill
Photographer   Roger Vlitos

The author, Julie Johnson, is a
health education consultant and
trainer, working with children,
parents, carers, teachers and
organisations such as Kidscape.

Contents

Introduction

Molly, Tom, Ali and Gary are friends. Each one of them is a member of a stepfamily. Families come in many different shapes and sizes. Stepfamilies are just one kind of family. The four friends will share their thoughts and feelings about having a stepparent, stepbrothers and stepsisters.

I see my mum and stepfamily at weekends.

I live with my stepmum and dad but I still see my natural mum.

I live with dad and my stepmum. I visit mum and my other stepfamily.

MOLLY

TOM

ALI

GARY

A stepfamily has its ups and downs, just like any family.

What are Stepfamilies?

Ali's dad and mum split up a few years ago. Ali's dad has a new partner called Kate. Kate is Ali's stepmum. Molly is telling Ali that being a member of a stepfamily is just like being in any family except that a stepfamily is made from two families, or one family and another grown-up.

In my stepfamily, there's me, my stepmum and my dad.

Jo is going to be your stepmum.

My stepfamily's almost big enough to be a football team!

You may have a stepparent...

4

...and stepbrothers and sisters.

What are Stepfamilies?

▼ Two Mums?

A stepfamily is the coming together of two adults, one or both of whom have children from a previous relationship. This means that you may have two mums – your natural mum and a stepmum. You can love them both in different ways.

It's great isn't it?

Yeah. I've never done this before.

◄ Little or Large?

A stepfamily may be quite large if your stepparent already has his or her own children. If both your parents have new partners, you may even have two stepfamilies!

Molly, how do people come to be in a stepfamily?

"Stepfamilies can happen for lots of reasons. Dad died when I was a baby. Then mum married Paul, my stepdad. My sister, mum and I went to live with Paul and his children. Ali has a stepfamily because her parents split up and her dad remarried."

5

Stepparents

Tom is telling Ali how much he enjoys his regular visits to see his mum, stepdad and stepbrothers. For most of the time, Tom lives with his natural dad and he gets on really well with his stepdad, too. But you may be more like Ali. It took her a long time to accept and to like her stepmum.

At first, I was cross with my stepmum for not being my natural mum. Now I know I can love them both.

No, I don't need any help.

I got on well with my stepdad straight away. He's really nice.

▼ I Miss My Mum

You may blame your stepparent for your natural parents splitting up. It's quite natural to feel like this. But try to remember that blaming people or feeling cross won't change the situation.

Will I ever get used to being a parent?

◀ Help!

For some grown-ups, becoming a stepparent is their first go at being a parent. Your stepparent may be worried about how you will all get on and if you will like him or her. Try to remember that grown-ups can feel nervous, too!

I don't want a new mum. I've already got one.

▶ I'm Confused!

You may feel confused if you love your natural parent, but also get on well with your new stepparent. Your natural mum or dad will always be special to you, but it is not wrong to care about your new parent. You can love people in different ways.

How can I love them both?

1. Mark thinks that his mum will stop loving Colin, his stepdad, if he is unfriendly to him.

2. Mark tells his mum that he doesn't like Colin because he's not his natural dad.

3. Colin tries to make friends with Mark but nothing seems to work.

Why is Mark being so unfriendly?

Mark misses his natural dad and is determined not to like Colin. He feels that Colin is trying to take the place of his dad. But being unfriendly to Colin will not make his mum and his natural dad get back together. Colin doesn't want to take the place of Mark's dad. He just wants to be a good friend to Mark.

▼ Two Lots of Parents!

If you live with your stepfamily you may also want to spend time with the parent from whom you live apart. This is not always possible, but remember that it's OK to love your stepparent and your natural parent.

I'll never like Paul because he's not my real dad.

◀ Feelings

If you find it very hard to accept or to like your stepparent, tell your other parent how you feel. Talking about your feelings doesn't make a problem go away, but it can help to make you feel better.

I do get on with my stepmum but it's so nice when I spend time with my mum.

Ali, how do you feel about having a mum and a stepmum?

"At first I didn't want to like Kate, my stepmum, because I missed my natural mum. But mum explained that I can love them in different ways. I still see my mum at weekends and she'll always be my mum. We have a great time together but I can have a good time with Kate, too."

Stepbrothers and Sisters

Molly and Tom both have stepbrothers and sisters, as well as their own natural brothers and sisters. It can take time to get used to having a stepbrother or sister. Remember that stepbrothers and sisters can fall out and be best of friends, just like any brothers and sisters!

They all look nice. I like my stepbrothers now, but when I first met them they just ignored me.

I found it hard at first, too, but we get on OK now. This photo is of us all on holiday.

I used to be the oldest. It's not fair.

It's not always easy to join in.

You may feel cross at all the changes.

▼ Quiet Time

You may sometimes want to spend some quiet time with your natural mum or dad, rather than always seeing him or her with your stepbrothers or sisters. There is nothing wrong in wanting to do this.

Nobody listens to me anymore.

◀ What About Me?

Having new stepbrothers and sisters can mean that you suddenly have to share your natural parent with lots of other people. This may make you feel fed up and a bit jealous, too.

▶ Feeling Left Out

If you feel left out or find it hard to get on with your stepbrothers or sisters, tell your natural parent or stepparent how you feel. He or she may not be able to make the problem go away immediately, but it can help to tell someone how you feel.

I can understand you feeling left out. I'm glad you told me.

1. Before Dan and his daughter, Rosie, moved in, Polly had her own room.

2. Polly felt really cross and fed up when Rosie moved into her room.

3. After a while, they got used to sharing a room. They even enjoyed it!

Why didn't Polly want to share her room with Rosie?

Polly didn't ask for a stepsister, but she got one, and she had to share her room with her! Sharing things with a stepbrother or sister can be hard if, like Polly, you have not had to do so before. It's not easy accepting situations which you have not chosen, but sometimes they work out better than you think!

▼ Why Can't I Choose?

Some stepbrothers and sisters hit it off straight away. It may be that you have not liked being an only child and now have someone to spend time with. A stepbrother or sister can become a good friend.

We don't want you to play with us.

◀ Help Make It Easy

If you are a member of a large family and a stepbrother or sister comes to visit or to stay with you, make an effort to include them in your games. You may not be best friends, but it helps to be friendly.

It's great having a sister to do things with now.

Molly, *tell us how you get on with your stepbrothers and stepsisters.*

"At first my sister and I didn't like them. But we all tried really hard and we get on most of the time, now. It's nice having Emma, who is older than I am. It's fun playing football with the boys but they can be a pain at times, just like all brothers."

Getting Used to Change

When Gary and his dad moved in with Gary's stepmum, Gary had to move school. He had to get used to a different way of doing things with his dad and stepmum, and another way of doing things with his mum and stepdad! Becoming part of a stepfamily can mean lots of change.

You may have to move house.

14

Things may be different.

▼ A New School!

A new family may also mean moving house and going to a new school. Going to a new school can be difficult, especially if you join in the middle of a term. All changes take a while to get used to.

Lauren is coming to live with us.

◀ It's Our House!

Sharing your home with a stepfamily can mean lots of changes. You may not like all of them. You may feel cross if no one asked you how you would feel about it. Try to remember that it's also strange for your new stepfamily.

▶ What Do I Call Her?

It can be difficult knowing what to call your stepparent. He or she is not your natural parent, and you may not want to call him or her dad or mum. It is a good idea to talk about it together so that you can decide what feels right for all of you.

What am I going to call my new mum?

1. Keith's dad has come to pick Keith up for his weekly day out together.

2. Keith enjoys being with his dad, who lives with Jan, his new partner.

3. Keith was upset when his dad said that he could not see him next Saturday.

Why was Keith disappointed?

Keith lives with his mum and sees his dad once a week. He enjoys being with his dad. The time you spend with the parent from whom you live apart is important. It can make you feel let down, upset and angry if he or she is unable to see you. This feeling is quite natural.

Getting Used to Change

▼ New Babies!

A new baby can mean lots of change, even if the baby is your natural brother or sister. But a new baby doesn't mean that your natural parent and your stepparent are going to stop loving you.

I think you've had enough sweets for one day!

But my mum never takes my sweets away.

◄ It's All Different Now!

You may find it difficult if your stepparent does not let you behave in the same way as your natural parent does. Try to tell both parents how you feel so you can all agree on what you are, or are not, allowed to do.

Susan is going to have a baby.

Gary, how did you cope with all the changes?

"To begin with, it was so confusing and I felt angry that everything had to change. Nothing was the same. But it was lots of change for everyone. Even though it was all scary, it was quite fun too."

Being a Family

Last week in class Tom and Molly were talking about what it means to be part of a family. They decided that in some ways being part of a stepfamily is not really that different from being part of any other family, except that you come together from two families.

My stepbrother made me some cakes for my birthday. Would you like one?

Yeah, as long as they taste better than the ones my stepsister makes!

You can go first.

There can be bad days...

18

...and there can be good days!

◀ Sharing

In all families everybody has to learn to get along. Some people find it easier than others. In a stepfamily, just like in any other family, there will be times when you get fed up with each other.

▶ Speak Up

Talking and listening to each other is important for all families. It can be especially important as members of a stepfamily get used to each other. Sorting out any difficulties is much easier if you talk to each other.

▲ Feeling Jealous

It is quite natural for you to feel a bit jealous of a stepbrother or stepsister. It may seem as if he or she is given special treatment by your parents. Try to remember that it takes time for everyone to get used to being in a stepfamily.

1. The Brooks family were trying to organise a day out.

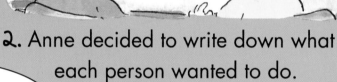

2. Anne decided to write down what each person wanted to do.

3. Anne's plan meant that everyone would be happy.

How did Anne manage to please everyone?

Anne's stepfamily all wanted to do something different. She decided to make a list of what each person wanted to do. That way, they worked out a plan which made everyone happy. Being part of a family is much easier and more fun if you all take time to think of each other.

▼ Good Times!

It can be great fun doing things together as a family and that means a stepfamily, too! You can still enjoy being part of a stepfamily, even if you only see your stepfamily from time to time.

It's your fault!

No, it's not. You did it!

Wah, wah!

◀ Not So Good Times!

All families have times when they get fed up with each other. But you'll feel much better about it if you don't stay cross for too long. Remember the good times and try to learn from the difficult times.

Tom, do you find it hard seeing your stepfamily only at weekends?

"It's not a problem. I love living with dad but it's great fun going to stay with my stepfamily, as well. It can take a while before I feel really at home when I go to visit my stepfamily, but after that it's just like being in any family."

Don't Forget . . .

Ali, what tips do you have about new stepparents?

"I was really upset at my parents splitting up. I didn't want to speak to Kate, my stepmum. But when I realised that my mum and dad were not going to get back together, I started to give Kate a chance. She's like a friend now."

Tom, what tips do you have for getting on with stepbrothers and sisters?

"Give them a chance because they probably feel as unsure about you as you do about them. Try not to decide straight away whether you like them or not. You may never be best of friends with them, but then again you may. You may even get on with them better than your natural brothers or sisters. And if you have any problems, talk about them."

Gary, what do you think about all the changes you have had to make?

"I was quite angry when dad first told me that I had to change school, move house and have a stepmum. But we had a talk and he said he was as nervous as I was about all the changes. It made it better because we both felt the same."

I'll be sharing my dad now, but I'll [hav]e a new mum as well.

I'll miss my old house.

But I'll write to my old friends.

I'm sure I'll like my new school.

Molly, have you got any tips for new stepfamilies?

"Try to accept the situation. It may be much better than you think. In any family, you need to work together and to talk about any problems. If you do feel uncomfortable, tell your natural parent or another grown-up who you trust."

Index

All the photographs in this book have been posed by models. The publishers would like to thank them all.